For when you stumble into this
lifetime

You will know how much I have loved
you,

Throughout every single one.

H

Come back to these pages.

Define You.

LOVE LETTERS

I need the most.

I need intelligent conversation.

I need chivalry.

I need support and to be cherished.

I need LOTS of love.

I need adventure and stability.

I need space enough to make my own choices but foundation enough to know I can count on the choices you make as well.

I need romance and reality.

The truth even when it hurts or differs from something you once said.

I need the absolute *whole* being you are, you have been, and you want to be and I need you to *expect* the same from me.

Unless these things are non-negotiable for both you and me,

we will remain an insatiable catastrophe.

TWO

I can feel it coming

Crush me into two

All this violence you create because you can't face you.

But I can see it coming

And I know who you are

And in the end, you do too but blame it on the dark

No one is coming to save you

You'll die knowing what was inside.

You'll never see it coming, following your pride.

The ending will be bitter and tasteless just for you.

I will end in one piece

But you

Will end in two

RUM RUNS RED

Here comes the gun

It kills me every time
The only words you say, make me want to die

Here comes the gun
I better open wide

BOOM

You pull the trigger and blow out my insides

GET YOURSELF TOGETHER

Always a bleeding mess

Don't you see it's your fault
You always cause the stress

Can't you see that I have needs your job is to fulfill

Keep your mouth quiet

And

Just

Hold

Still

PROMETHEUS

The buzzing of the bumbles

The falling of the leaves

The synchronistic melodies with the wind in breeze

Crossing all the x's
Tic in the tac toes

All the words we never speak but somehow always know

In all ways it is everything
But nothings not that far

Encompassing creations mapped out beneath the stars

To see beyond the hiding
To feel despite the knife
To taste the blood around you, but also that inside
The smell all of the colors
Hearing day and night

The existential crisis of death
and all of life

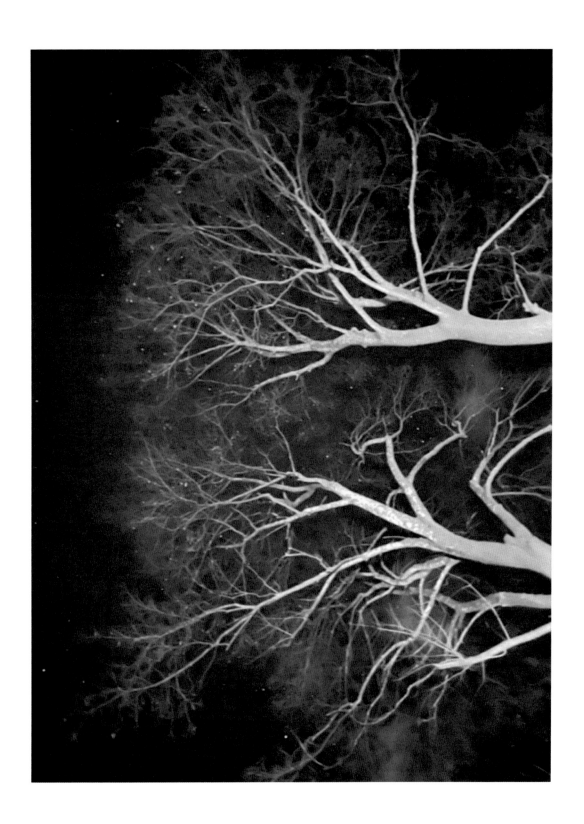

THE WAITING

I wait for you

You wait for me

I see you

You see me

Without words or commentary

Just you

Just me

Voiceless glee

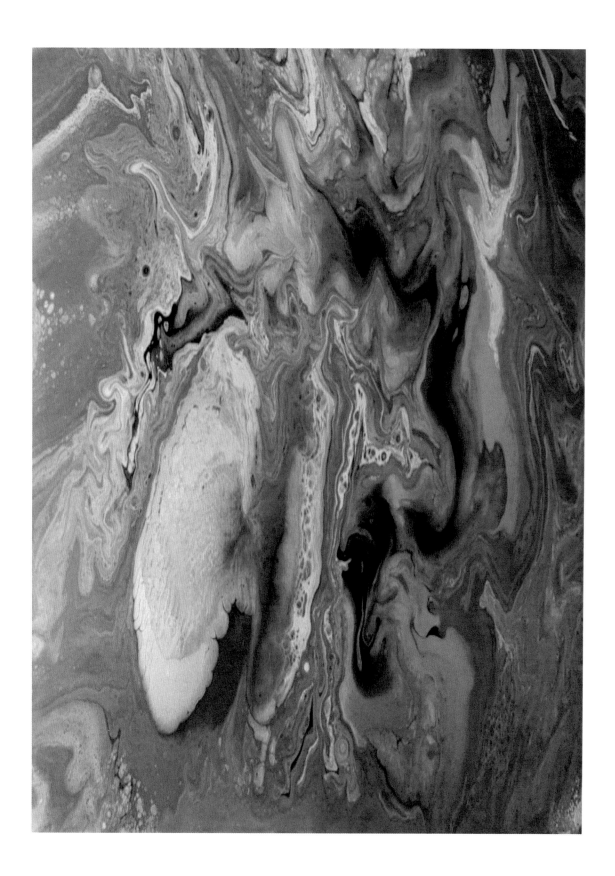

MIRRORED SIDES OF PILLOWS

How are you who I am?

Yet something I could never be.

A piece of my own self

Reflecting

Mirrored back at me.

So much to gain
So much to lose but here we are, and we still choose

Not in a dream but here in life
We mix our hearts
Inspired strife's

A flower planted in a grave

We'll know what comes once it rains

PRIMA BALLERINA

A perfect Arabella

A second pointed toe

Another broken wrist to match the ankle down below

The grace in all the movements each hand has once it grasps

The art of our love dying as blood pours from every crevasse

Oh, the ballerina I have come to be

Tattered and torn from all angles

But the dance is never complete

Forever dancing for you
As you bring me to my knees

The song that never ends

The song that keeps you pleased.

VULTURE

Encircling the body that you left for me.

Not a real life, but you can see me breathe.

Not a true person, but an idol on the wall.

The damage man can do

When he has to conquer it all.

THE CHANGING

Changes

Arrangements

Are you dazed yet?

All this movement is shameless

Who are they judge you worse than you judge yourself

And whose ever there when your surrounded by all your doubts

I see you in the mirror

I see you on your phone

All the stories adding up just shows that you're alone.

And trust me I know the feeling

But you, you hide it well

The road to hell is paved with good intentions

Could you tell?

Didn't you tell?

All the souls your saving

But cannot save yourself.

MIDAS

Black and blue and purple

The only colors that I see.

Black and blue and purple my favorite colors they must be.

Black and blue and purple and I guess sometimes there's red.

Hide it on the outside so it only seeps into your head.

Black and red and purple and don't forget the blue,

Not only on the outside

Now it lives inside of you.

TIC TAC TOE

The body keeps the score

I guess I'd say that's true.

But what's the body keep if it doesn't come back to you?

And who's your body's really when it doesn't feel like yours?

And who can really help you when you don't know your source?

Oh where, oh where are you hiding flesh?

Where, oh where could you be?

I've looked out in the forest and in the bed, we sleep.

Underneath the covers and out there in the fields,

I don't think that you're hiding, but I can't find you here.

I know that skin will wither and in time fall apart but I know my organs need you, especially - - - - - - -

My heart.

So, if somehow you can find me

Lead me back to where you stay

I'd fall right back into you and never go away.

I've learned without your comfort I morph but into steel.

and if I am but an object then how can I be real?

ARE WE THERE YET?

There is wisdom in the wild

And discipline in the untamed.

A contradicting statement but the truth remains the same.

For how can we be whole without knowing rules are games

The only way to win is not to even play.

So, come with me dear flower.

Your roots will always grow.

As long as you keep them watered with the strength to trust the unknown.

Oh, my dear sweet child they'll have so much to say

But what will those words matter when you're in the grave?

Ignite your fiercest fire.

Unleash your uninhibited flame.

Though the world will always judge you

Your soul will never shake .

A special thank you to all the incredibly talented and ethereal artist who helped create the next piece to this literary puzzle.

Collaborating from all parts of this world and all pieces of our hearts.

Pages 5, 17, 35, 40 Matt Troop

Pages 6,7,12,13,22,23,32,33, 38,39 Quray Clarke @okayclarkee

Page 8 Julian Hamilton @daadjazz_arts_

Page 10 Clea Rojas @kdeclea

Page 14 @yzzhprum_

Page 16 Lauren Diamond @lauren.diamond16

Page 19 Mark Seltzer

Page 21 Jade Ellen

Page 24 Nakayama @kazamatt

Page 27 Michelle Dickinson

Pages 28, 31 Mackenzie Fitzgerald @kenziegraves

Page 36 Christina Tremblay @chrissytremblay

Pages 2, 42 were created with some very special earth angels Harper, Madelyn and Caleb with Sophia in spirit.

Made in the USA
Middletown, DE
26 October 2023

41410019R00024